# GRANDMA LAI GOON REMEMBERS

Text © 2002 by Ann Morris

Photographs and illustrations © 2002 by Peter Linenthal

Designed by Carolyn Eckert

Other photographs courtesy of © the Leong family: pp. 7, 10, 14, 32;

© Horace Bristol/Corbis: p. 13 (left); © Brown Brothers: p. 13 (right)


Library of Congress Cataloging-in-Publication Data


Morris, Ann, 1930-

Grandma Lai Goon remembers: a Chinese-American family story/

Ann Morris; photographs and illustrations by Peter Linenthal.

p. cm. — (What was it like, Grandma?)

Summary:  A Chinese-American grandmother relates family and cultural

history from her life in Guangzhou, China to her grandchildren.

ISBN 0-7613-2314-7 (lib. bdg.)

1. China—Social life and customs—Juvenile literature. [1. China—

Social life and customs.] I. Linenthal, Peter, ill. II. Title.


DS775.2 .M67 2002          951.05—dc21          2001044085


The Millbrook Press, Inc.

2 Old New Milford Road

Brookfield, Connecticut 06804

www.millbrookpress.com

*What Was It Like, Grandma?*

# GRANDMA LAI GOON
# ❀ REMEMBERS

*A Chinese-American Family Story*

**Ann Morris**

**Photographs and Illustrations by Peter Linenthal**

**The Millbrook Press**
**Brookfield, Connecticut**

Allyson, age eight, and Daniel, age nine, greet Grandma Lai Goon.

**"Well, how was school today?" Grandma Lai Goon asks as she meets Allyson and Daniel at the bus stop.**

"Great," reply the children. Excitedly they tell their grandmother about their day at school. Daniel shows her a project he has been working on.

Allyson and Daniel live with their older sister, Sarah, and their parents in an apartment near San Francisco's Chinatown. Mary and Wilson, their parents, work all day in the city as social workers, helping people solve problems.

**Grandma Lai Goon takes care of Allyson and Daniel before and after school.**

**Grandma Lai Goon lives in an apartment around the corner from the children and their parents.**

She has lived there for many years. It is the same apartment that Mary grew up in. Besides Mary, Lai Goon has two daughters and one son. Mary was the youngest.

**In Chinese, "Lai" means beautiful. But the children call Lai Goon "Paw Paw," which means grandmother.**

Lai Goon in her kitchen as a young woman

Allyson and Daniel enjoy spending time with Grandma Lai Goon. Sometimes she shows them her family album. As they look through the old family photographs together, she tells them stories about her life.

Lai Goon doesn't speak English. She speaks to the children in Chinese, the language she learned when she was growing up.

岗头里

防洪闸

入村小桥 →

4/25

The full name of the village is Sam Fow Dic Hoy, but most people call it Dic Hoy.

Grandma Lai Goon was born in Dic Hoy, a small village in Canton (Guangzhou), China, more than seventy years ago.

# Lai Goon tells the children that the village was only ten blocks long.

The village had no electricity, so there was no TV, radio, nor movies. Most of the villagers lived in small homes made of clay bricks. Because there wasn't enough room in the homes for the whole family to sleep, all the girls of the town slept in a separate house.

There were no cows in the village, so there was no milk. "Our meals were mainly rice, with a little fish and some vegetables — eggplant, squash, and greens," says Lai Goon. "And sometimes we didn't have enough to eat."

Most of the people in Lai Goon's village were poor farmers. They raised rice in paddies, or fields, around the town. The rice attracted rats. The people kept cats to chase away the rats.

# Lai Goon's whole family worked in their rice paddy.

Lai Goon worked in the paddy beside her mother. One of her jobs was to plant rice. She used her feet to pound the soil in place. Lai Goon did not stop for lunch. She would work until three in the afternoon and then return home to eat. Later she would go to the riverbank to collect clams.

**Chinese rice paddies**

**These people are harvesting rice just as Lai Goon**

**used to do.**

**Lai Goon as a young woman (sitting center)**

**with some friends and relatives**

There were six people in Grandma Lai Goon's family — Lai Goon, her father and mother, two brothers, and one sister.

"My father was very strict," Lai Goon tells Allyson and Daniel. "He expected us to have good manners. He always reminded us to say good morning to our elders before going out to play or work." But she also remembers that he was very kind. "He always took good care of me when I was sick," she says, "and gave me medicines made from herbs and plants."

**When Grandma Lai Goon was little, her brothers went to school, but she and her sisters did not.**

Only boys went to school then, so that they could get jobs when they grew up. Girls were expected to raise families, so they did not go to school. But Lai Goon wanted to go to school.

When Lai Goon was seventeen, she earned a little money selling clams. Then she could afford to go to school for a short time where she learned to read and write.

When Grandma Lai Goon was nineteen, she left Dic Hoy to find work in another town. Before long she met a young man, Chuck Woon, and they got married. Soon after, Chuck Woon left China to find work in San Francisco. In 1949 Lai Goon joined him. She got a job in a sewing factory and began to raise a family. Even though she and Chuck Woon didn't have much money, they made sure that their children went to college.

Lai Goon is retired now, but she keeps busy. She takes care of Allyson and Daniel. And every morning she does tai chi, Chinese exercises that she learned ten years ago. These movements help strengthen the body and the mind.

# Many people say that Lai Goon is so good at tai chi that she could be a teacher!

When they come home from school, Grandma Lai Goon often teaches Allyson and Daniel skills she learned when she was growing up.

**Allyson and Daniel learn to write Chinese words with a special brush and black ink.**

This kind of writing is called *calligraphy*.

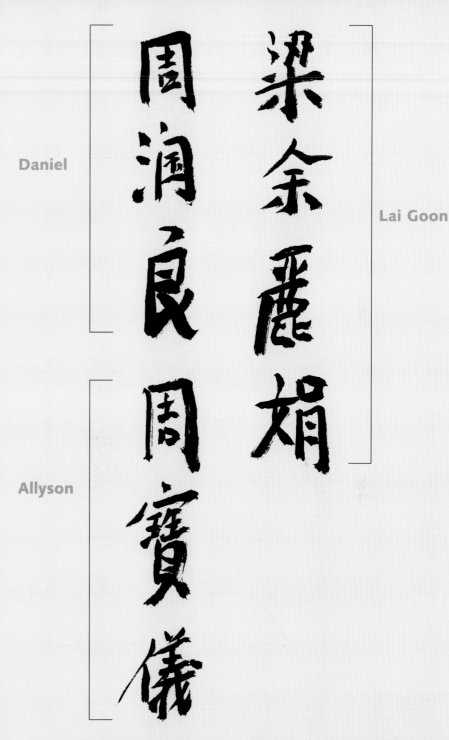

Daniel

Lai Goon

Allyson

**This is *Daniel*, *Allyson*, and *Lai Goon* in Chinese.**

# Grandma Lai Goon also teaches her grandchildren how to make Chinese dolls.

"This is the way we made the dolls in Dic Hoy," explains Lai Goon. "We used incense sticks for the body," Lai Goon explains. "For heads, we used black clay from the riverbank where I went digging for clams. For hair we used the silky roots of rice plants, and for clothes we sewed together pieces of old cloth."

## Chinese Dolls

When Allyson and Daniel make their dolls, they use different materials. You can make the dolls, too.

### HERE IS WHAT YOU NEED:

Ice cream craft sticks

Clay

Cornstalk silk or yarn

Scraps from old clothes

Glue

Needle and thread

Scissors

Pencil

### HERE IS WHAT YOU DO:

1. Shape the head out of clay. Use a pencil to draw eyes, a nose, and a mouth.

2. Put the pop sticks in the clay; then let the clay dry.

4. Glue the corn silk on the head.

5. Make clothes from the cloth scraps and sew them in place.

# ACTIVITY

## Pebble Game (Chinese "Jacks")

### OBJECT OF THE GAME:

Using only one hand, throw one pebble into the air, pick up the remaining pebbles, and then catch the original pebble before it hits the ground.

### TO BEGIN:

Place the five pebbles in the palm of your hand. Flip the pebbles so they land on the top of your hand. Then flip them back into your palm. The player who catches the most pebbles goes first. A player's turn ends when the player cannot complete a round.

### ROUND 1

Toss the five pebbles in front of you. Pick one pebble to use as your "tosser." Using only one hand, throw your tosser into the air and quickly pick up one of the remaining pebbles, catching the tosser before it hits the ground. Repeat until you have picked up all the pebbles.

### ROUND 2

Toss the five pebbles. Pick one pebble to use as your "tosser." Using only one hand, throw your tosser into the air and quickly pick up two pebbles, catching the tosser before it hits the ground. Repeat again to pick up the remaining two pebbles.

### ROUND 3

Toss the five pebbles. Pick one pebble to use as your "tosser." Using only one hand, throw your tosser into the air and quickly pick up one pebble, catching the tosser before it hits the ground. Toss again to pick up the remaining three pebbles.

### ROUND 4

Toss the five pebbles. Pick one pebble to use as your "tosser." Using only one hand, throw your tosser into the air and quickly pick up all four pebbles, catching the tosser before it hits the ground.

### FINAL ROUND

Holding all five pebbles in your hand, flip the pebbles onto the other side of your hand and back again into your palm. If you don't catch the pebbles, the next player takes a turn.

The player who completes this round wins. However, if any other player gets to this round, then the player who catches the most pebbles in the final round wins.

**When Grandma Lai Goon was a girl, she played a pebble game that is something like American jacks.**

It uses stones instead of jacks and a ball.

Allyson and Daniel enjoy playing Chinese "jacks" with Lai Goon, their mother, and their older sister, Sarah.

# Grandma Lai Goon is a good cook.

Her specialty Chinese buns are called "bow." Sometimes the children help her make bow, tasting bits of it as they cook.

# A DO-IT-TOGETHER ACTIVITY

## "Bow" (Chinese Buns)

Makes 24 buns.

**SAFETY TIP:**

If you try this, get an adult to help.

**HERE IS WHAT YOU NEED:**

| | |
|---|---|
| 1 | package active dry yeast |
| 3 | tablespoons sugar |
| 1/2 | cup lukewarm water |
| 1 | cup very hot milk |
| 1 | cup mashed potatoes |
| 1/2 | cup shortening |
| 1/2 | cup sugar |
| 2 | eggs |
| 1 | teaspoon salt |
| 6 | cups all-purpose flour |

**EGG MIXTURE**

1 egg yolk mixed with 1 teaspoon of milk

**FILLING**

Chinese sausage or black bean paste

**HERE IS WHAT YOU DO:**

1. In a mixing bowl dissolve the yeast and 3 tablespoons of sugar in the lukewarm water.

2. Heat the milk in a pan. Stir in the mashed potatoes, shortening, 1/2 cup sugar, eggs, and salt.

3. Add the potato mixture to the dissolved yeast. Stir in 2 cups of flour, and mix well.

4. Add the remaining 4 cups of flour, and mix until the dough is easy to handle.

5. Turn the dough onto a lightly floured board, and knead it until it is smooth and elastic (about 10 minutes).

6. Place the dough in a greased bowl.

7. Cover the bowl, and let the dough rise in a warm place until it doubles in size (about 1 hour).

8. Punch down the dough; then let it rise again until it doubles in size.

9. Shape the dough into buns, and add the filling.

10. Preheat the oven to 400°F.

11. Put the buns on a cookie sheet, and let them rise until they double in size.

12. Brush the buns with the egg mixture. Then bake for 15 to 25 minutes, or steam in a steamer.

The best part about bow is eating them! "They are so delicious," says Allyson.

# The whole family enjoys Lai Goon's bow.

Allyson, Mary, and Lai Goon

Grandma Lai Goon and the children play cards.

# ALL ABOUT MY FAMILY

## Would you like to know about your family? Here are some things you can do.

### INTERVIEWS

You will find out many interesting things about your relatives by interviewing them. Ask them questions about their childhood—where they lived, what they liked best to do and to eat, what they read and studied in school. Find out, too, how things are different today from when they were young. Use a tape recorder to record your questions and their answers.

### FAMILY ALBUM

Ask your relatives for pictures of themselves. Put all the pictures in an album. Write something you have learned about each person under his or her picture.

### FAMILY TREE

All of us have many relatives. Some of us are born into the family. Others are related by marriage or have been adopted. You can make a family tree that looks like the one on the next page to show who belongs to your family.

# LEONG FAMILY TREE

Lai Goon

Chuck Woon

Mary

Daniel and Allyson

Wilson

Sarah